Religious Life Style in Different Young Social Groups

Ankit Patel

Createspace

An Amazon Company

ISBN-13: 978-1494800185

ISBN-10: 1494800187

DEDICATION

Humanity
Because I believe it is.

CONTENTS

	Acknowledgments	i
1.	Key Words	1
2.	Introduction	2
3.	Religious In India	4
4.	Review Of Literature	8
5	Methodology	10
5.1	Objectives	10
5.2	Hypothesis	11
5.3	Sample	11
5.4	Variable	12
5.5	Tool And Techniques	12
10.	Result And Discussions	13
11	Charts	22
12	Conclusion	26
13	Suggestions	27
14	Reference	28

ACKNOWLEDGMENTS

I thank the department of Psychology, Sardar Patel University,
Vallabh Vidyanagar, Gujarat, India, especially my master,
Dr. Suresh Makvana for the importance they
place on innovation in research and the
encouragement to do more.

I also thank the staff members of the Psychology department for
their support, insights and constructive suggestions.

1. KEY WORDS

Christian, Muslim, Hindu, Male, Female, Religious

2. INTRODUCTION

There are numerous definitions of religion. Only a few are stated here. The typical Dictionary definition of religion utters "belief or worship of god or gods" or the service and worship of god or gods or the supernatural.

Edward Burnett Taylor defined religion as "the belief in spiritual things as a system of symbols he described it as the belief in a supreme deity or judgment after death or idolatry and so on. The belief in spiritual beings exists in all known societies. The sociologist Durkheim defined religion as system of beliefs and practices related to sacred things, they can be a rock, trees a spring, a pebble, a pace of world, a house- in a word anything can be sacred.

Psychologist William James defined religion as the feelings, arts and experiences of individual man in solitude. He considers it as divine, by the term divine. James meant any object that is godlike, whether it is concert or not.

Thus religion is a set of belief in god, divine, spirit or deity. It is individual's personal experience according to William James (psychologist).

The development of religion has taken different forms in different culture. Some religions emphasis on belief while others on practice some religions claim to be Universal. Some religions emphasis on the Subjective experience of religious individual I in many places, religion have been associated with Public institution. Such as education, hospitals, family, government political hierarchies.

One modern academic concept of religion is social constructivism which suggests all spiritual practices and worship. There are different religions in the world. The five largest groups of world population estimate to account for 5 billion people. The distribution of world population in five major religions is as under.

Five major religion	Adherent in 2000	% world population
Christianity	2-0 billion	33%
Islam	1-2 billion	16%
Hinduism	811 million	13.4%
Chinese Folk religion	385 million	6.4%
Buddhism	360 million	5.0%

In this present research researcher wants to compare the religious attitudes of Christian students, Muslim students and Hindu students.

3. RELIGIOUS IN INDIA

Religion in India is characterized by a diversity of religious beliefs and practices. India is the birthplace of four of the world's major religions; namely Hinduism, Buddhism, Jainism and Sikhism. Throughout India's history, religion has been an important part of the country's culture. Religious diversity and religious tolerance are both established in the country by the law and custom. A vast majority of Indians, (over 93%) associate themselves with a religion.

According to the 2001 census, 80.5% of the population of India practise Hinduism. Islam (13.4%), Christianity (2.3%), Sikhism (1.9%), Buddhism (0.8%) and Jainism (0.4%) are  the other major religions followed by the people of India. There are also numerous minor tribal traditions, though these have been affected by major religions such as Hinduism, Buddhism and Christianity.

The amount of diversity in the religious belief systems of India today, is a result of both the existence of many native religions and also, the assimilation and social integration of religions brought to the region by travelers, immigrants, traders, and even invaders and conquerors such as the Mughals.

Zoroastrianism and Judaism also have an ancient history in India, and each has several thousands of Indian adherents. India has the largest population of people adhering to Zoroastrianism (i.e. Parsis and Iranis) and Bahá'í Faith in the world, even though these religions are not native to India. Many other world religions also have a relationship with Indian spirituality, such as the Baha'i faith which recognizes Buddha and Krishna as manifestations of the God Almighty.

The Indian Diaspora in the West has popularized many aspects of Hindu philosophy such as yoga, meditation, Ayurvedic medicine, divination, karma, and reincarnation. The influence of Indian religions has been significant all over the world. Several organizations, such as the Hare Krishna movement, the Brahma Kumaris, the Ananda Marga, and others have spread Indian spiritual beliefs and practices.

The Muslim population of India is the third largest in the world. India also has the third largest Shia population in the world. The shrines of some of the most famous saints of Sufism, like Moinuddin Chishti and Nizamuddin Auliya, are found in India, and attract visitors from all over the world. India is also home to some of the most famous monuments of Islamic architecture, such as the Taj Mahal and the Qutb Minar. Civil matters related to the community are dealt with by the Muslim Personal Law, and constitutional amendments in 1985 established its primacy in family matters.

The Constitution of India declares the nation to be a secular republic that must uphold the right of citizens to freely worship and propagate any or no religion or faith. The Constitution of India also declares the right to freedom of religion to be a fundamental right.

Population of Indian religion:

(2011, report of Government of India)

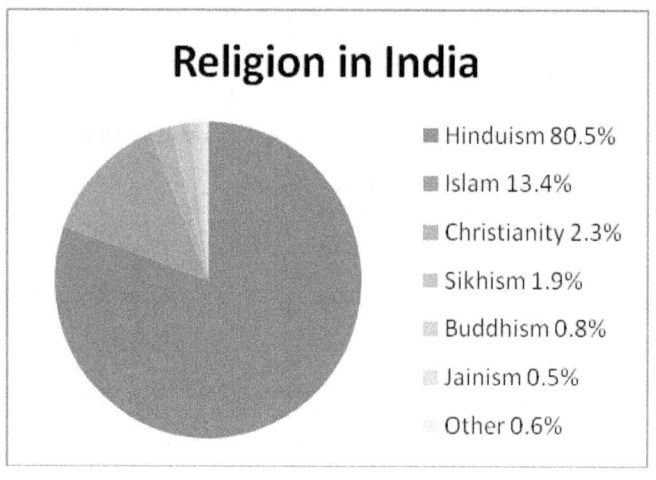

Religious group	Population %	Growth (1991 to 2001)	Ratio of Sex (In Total)	Literacy %	Work Participation %	Sex Ratio *Rural	Sex Ratio **Urban	Sex Ratio ***Child
Hindu	80.46%	20.3%	931	65.1%	40.4%	944	894	925
Muslim	13.43%	29.3%	936	59.1%	31.3%	953	907	950
Christian	2.34%	22.6%	1009	80.3%	39.7%	1001	1026	964
Sikh	1.87%	18.2%	893	69.4%	37.7%	895	886	786
Buddhist	0.77%	18.2%	953	72.7%	40.6%	958	944	942
Animist and others	0.72%	103.1%	992	47.0%	48.4%	995	966	976
Jain	0.41%	26.0%	940	94.1%	32.9%	937	941	870

(Chart of Indian religious communities, Characteristics of religious groups in 2001 census)

4. REVIEW OF LITERATURE

[1] Joseph Castleberry on religions - Based higher education.

President Joseph Castleberry of northwest University (WD) of Kirkland discussed what it is like to religiously Based institution of higher education, we discuss the change NU recently made from college to university. Dr.Joseph's pathway to his position as president as well as the various challenges a small religious University faces in recognizing students and faculty and maintain high level of scholarship while staying true to one's religious mission (July 7th 2013).

[2] Rebecca shah on Religion & The enterprising poor in India.

Rebecca shah of George Town University's Berkley's center discusses her research on how religions belief and predict affects the economic process of the enterprising poor in India. We review particular challenges facing women entrepreneurs in the poorest neighborhood of Bangalore (5.6 2013).

[3] Ann wainscot on the Political Islam in morocco.

What explains political Islam Particularly variant of this movement in morocco? Ann wainscot, graduate student at the University of Florida's advances a novel explanation relating educational reform. In an attempt to forestall all advancing latest in society during 1960 and 1970, the rule of king hasan promote greater. Islamic education within the – Country's public school system that has the unintentional consequence of creating new space for Islamists. This is not the only reason for the emergence of new Islamic movement (July 16th 2013).

4] Carolyn Warner on Religion and Generosity.

Why religions motivate generosity? The answer given by Prof Carolyn Warner (ASU) who is in a cross – faith and why religious individuals give money and time to others.

Catholic and Muslims in Ireland and Turkey, using both person to person Interviews and experimental design to see it there are differences across these faith traditions she and her team discovered that Catholics tend to be motivate by "Love of God" and Muslims give out of a duty to god I It still remains to be decided when Individual are motivate to help anther by the effort of religious organizations or of their own account (June 9th 2013).

5. METHODOLOGY

5.1 Objectives:

Many important objectives of this research work are mentioned here.

   i. Main objective of this research is to find out the difference of religious attitude in different social groups.

   ii. Another objective of this research is that which social group has better life style.

   iii. To study the religious life style of males and females is also the aim of this research.

   iv. To know about the religious attitude of different internal social group.

   v. How the factor of social group affect, on religious attitude is also the purpose of this research.

   vi. Another aim of this research is to know the causes of different religious attitude.

   vii. Suggestions about the healthy and happy religious life for the whole society and world.

5.2 Hypothesis:

1) SAI (SAI means higher level of spirituality)

   There is no any difference in spirituality of Hindu, Christian and Muslim.

2) EWBS (Grater existential well being)

   There is no any difference in EWBS of different social groups.

3) NRCOPE (Lower levels of negative religious coping)

   There is no any difference in Hindu, Christian, and Muslim's NRCOPE.

4) MHLC (Greater locus control)

   All the three social groups are not different in MHLC.

5) There is no any significant difference in religious attitude of males and females.

5.3 Sample:

For present study 120 students were selected randomly from different cities and village of Gujarat State (India). Distribution of sample is mention in this table.

Social Group	Male	Female	Total
Hindu	20	20	**40**
Christian	20	20	**40**
Muslim	20	20	**40**
*	**Grand total**		**120**

5.4 Variables:

Different variables are used for verification of purpose. Here is the table of variable.

Independent Variable	Dependent Variable
Hindi	Religious attitude
Christian	"
Muslim	"
Male	"
Female	"

5.5 Tools and Techniques:

To measure and evaluate the entire hypothesis Spiritual Attitude Inventory of USA (HEEM) was used. This research is for only young people. The young students between 19 to 22 years were selected randomly from different parts of Gujarat State (India).

To collect the data for this research the researcher visited himself every place. After establishing the rapport researcher has given inventory to students. All the students responded very well Data was analyzed according to SPI's Scoring key. Scientific result was found out by researcher.

6. RESULT DISCUSSIONS

1. SAI :

Table No-1.1: This table indicates result of 't' test, between Hindus and Christians.

Table no	Group	Mean	SD	SEM	t	Levels
1	Hindu	98.70	9.98	1.58	1.3487	0.01
	Christian	102.08	12.28	1.94		NS

There is no any difference in SAI of Hindu group and Christian group. 't' is not significant at 0.01 level.

Table No-1.2:

Table no	Group	Mean	SD	SEM	t	Levels
2	Christian	102.08	12.28	1.94	1.8777	0.01
	Muslim	97.60	8.74	1.38		NS

This table indicates that Christians and Muslims do not differ in SAI. 't' is not significant.

Table No-1.3:

Table no	Group	Mean	SD	SEM	T	Levels
3	Hindu	98.70	9.98	1.58	0.5244	0.01
	Muslim	97.60	8.74	1.38		NS

Social groups of Hindus and Muslim are equal in SAI. Proved by 't' test's result.

2. **DUREL:**

Table No-2.1:

Table no	Group	Mean	SD	SEM	T	Levels
4	Hindu	17.55	4.47	0.71	4.9588	0.01
	Christian	22.25	3.99	0.63		sig

This is very important and notable for whole research work only these two groups have significant difference.

Now you can watch in table No-2.1 Social group of Hindu and Christian are significantly different from each other.

Hindu's group having stronger religious attitude than Christians.

Table No-2.2: Above table mention religious attitude of Christians and Muslims.

Table no	Group	Mean	SD	SEM	t	Levels
5	Christian	22.25	3.99	0.63	2.7086	0.01
	Muslim	23.00	11.91	1.88		Ns

In this table there is no difference in both groups life style.

Table No-2.3:

Table no	Group	Mean	SD	SEM	t	Levels
6	Hindu	17.55	4.47	0.71	0.3775	0.01
	Muslim	23.00	11.91	1.88		Ns

This table also indicates that there is no difference between Hindus and Muslims life style.

3. EWBS:

Table No-3.1: This table indicates well being of Hindus and Christian group.

Table no	Group	Mean	SD	SEM	t	Levels
7	Hindu	41.63	7.55	1.19	1.3165	0.01
	Christian	39.55	6.51	1.03		Ns

't' is not significant in the table. So both groups are equal in well being.

Table No-3.2:

Table no	Group	Mean	SD	SEM	t	Levels
8	Christian	39.55	6.51	1.03	0.2378	0.01
	Muslim	39.90	6.66	1.05		Ns

There is no any difference in well being of Christian and Muslim. Proved by 't' Test.

Table No-3.3:

Table no	Group	Mean	SD	SEM	T	Levels
9	Hindu	41.63	7.55	1.19	1.0839	0.01
	Muslim	39.90	6.66	1.05		Ns

Here is also same result of both groups, which mentions in previous tables.

4. NRCOPE:

Means Negative Religious Attitude.

Table No-4.1:

Table no	Group	Mean	SD	SEM	t	Levels
10	Hindu	24.10	3.78	0.60	1.6363	0.01
	Christian	22.70	3.87	0.61		Ns

This table indicates negative religious attitude of Hindus and Christians.

't' test is not significant in both group, means there is no any difference.

Table No-4.2:

Table no	Group	Mean	SD	SEM	t	Levels
11	Christian	22.70	3.87	0.61	0.3786	0.01
	Muslim	22.38	3.81	0.60		Ns

Christians and Muslim do not differ in negative religious attitude. Proved by 't' test.

Table No-4.3:

Table no	Group	Mean	SD	SEM	T	Levels
12	Hindu	24.10	3.78	0.60	2.0331	0.01
	Muslim	22.38	3.81	0.60		Ns

Hindu's social group and Muslim's social group are equal in negative life style, which is mentioned in this table.

5. MHLC:

Means greater locus of Control.

Table NO-5.1:

Table no	Group	Mean	SD	SEM	t	Levels
13	Hindu	16.10	3.36	0.53	0.4948	0.01
	Christian	16.58	5.05	0.80		Ns

In this group there is an impression of locus of control. Present table indicates locus of control of Hindus and Christians.

There is no any difference in both groups. 't' is calculated for this purpose

Table-5.2:

Table no	Group	Mean	SD	SEM	t	Levels
14	Christian	16.58	5.05	0.80	2.2174	0.01
	Muslim	14.18	4.62	0.73		Ns

This table also indicates that there is no difference in both social groups.

Table-5.3:

Table no	Group	Mean	SD	SEM	t	Levels
15	Hindu	16.10	3.36	0.53	2.1307	0.01
	Muslim	14.18	4.62	0.73		Ns

Hindus and Muslim are equal in locus of control. Result of 't' test supported this result.

6. Table No-6: These tables indicate total difference of Males and Females of whole social group.

Table no	Group	Mean	SD	SEM	t	Levels
16	Male	99.45	11.16	1.44	0.0086	0.01
	Female	99.47	9.94	1.28		NS

For this 't' test was used which proved that Females and Males have same religious life style.

7. **SAI** (**Interactional effects**): Table seven indicates internal effects of religious attitude of SAI. Especially for Males and Females.

Table No-7.1:

Table no	Group	Mean	SD	SEM	t	Levels
17	Hindu Male	98.60	12.26	2.74	0.0625	0.01 Ns
	Hindu Female	98.80	7.37	1.65		

This table indicates SAI of Hindu Males and Hindu Females. 't' test proves that there is no any difference between males and Females SAI.

Table No 7.2: Christian Males and Females having same spiritual attitude

Table no	Group	Mean	SD	SEM	t	Levels
18	Christian Male	102.20	11.07	2.47	0.0635	0.01 Ns
	Christian Female	101.95	13.68	3.06		

Table No-7.3: Muslim Males and Females are also equal n spiritual life.

Table no	Group	Mean	SD	SEM	t	Levels
19	Muslim Male	97.55	10.08	2.25	0.0357	0.01 Ns
	Muslim Female	97.65	7.43	1.66		

Table No-7.4: There is no any significant difference in SAI of Hindus males and Christian Females.

Table no	Group	Mean	SD	SEM	t	Levels
20	Hindu Male	98.60	12.26	2.74	0.8157	0.01 Ns
	Christian Female	101.95	13.68	3.06		

Table No-7.5: Christian male and Muslim Females have no any difference in SAI.

Table no	Group	Mean	SD	SEM	t	Levels
21	Christian Male	102.20	11.07	2.47	1.5266	0.01 Ns
	Muslim Female	97.65	7.43	1.66		

Table No-7.6: This table also proves that there is no any difference in SAI of Muslim males and Christian Females.

Table no	Group	Mean	SD	SEM	t	Levels
22	Muslim Male	97.55	10.08	2.25	1.1582	0.01 Ns
	Christian Female	101.95	13.68	3.06		

Table No-7.7: There is also no any difference in SAI of Muslim male and Hindu Females.

Table no	Group	Mean	SD	SEM	t	Levels
23	Muslim Male	97.55	10.08	2.25	0.4479	0.01 Ns
	Hindu Female	98.80	7.37	1.65		

Table No-7.8 and 7.9: Both the tables indicate that all the four social groups have same SAI.

Table no	Group	Mean	SD	SEM	t	Levels
24	Hindu Male	98.60	12.26	2.74	0.2964	0.01 Ns
	Muslim Female	97.65	7.43	1.66		
Table no	Group	Mean	SD	SEM	t	Levels
25	Christian Male	102.20	11.07	2.47	1.1437	0.01 Ns
	Hindu Female	98.80	7.37	1.65		

7. CHARTS

Christian, Hindu, Muslim groups from SAI.

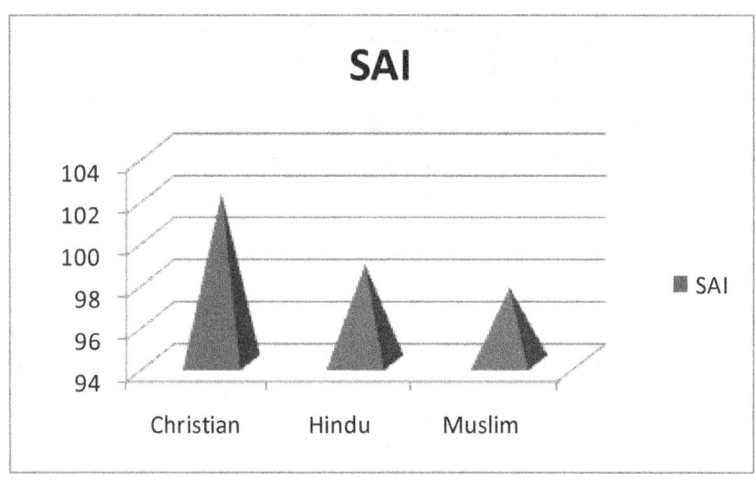

Figure 1

Christian, Muslim and Hindu group from DUREL.

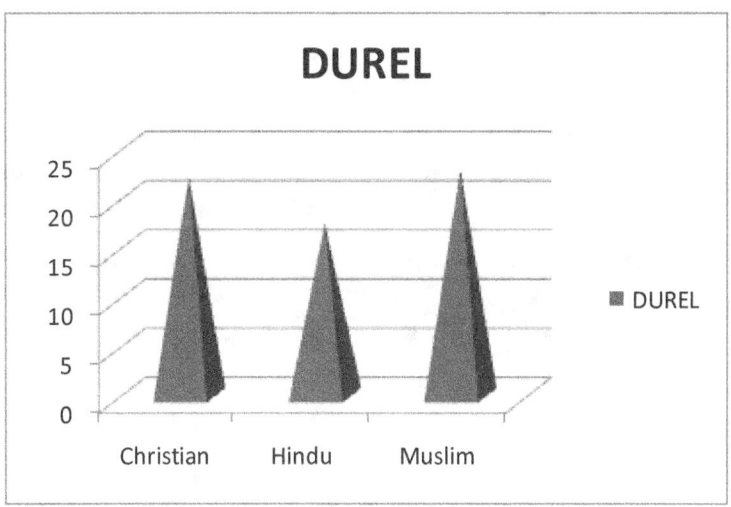

Figure 2

Christian, Muslim and Hindu group from EWBS.

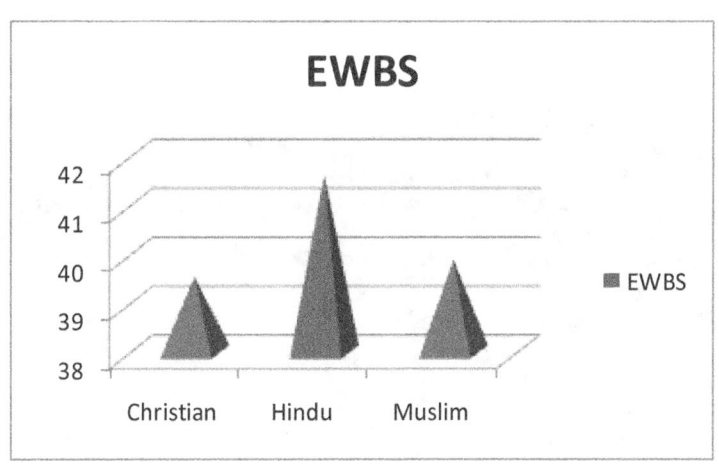

Figure 3

Christian, Muslim and Hindu group from NRCOPE.

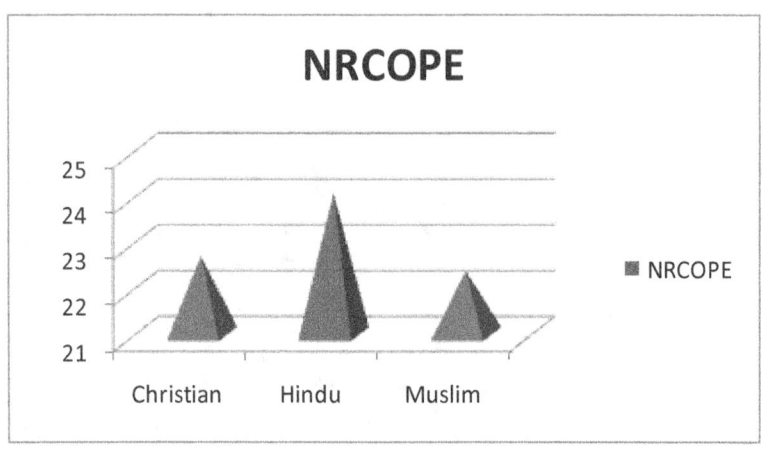

Figure 4

Christian, Muslim and Hindu group from MHLC.

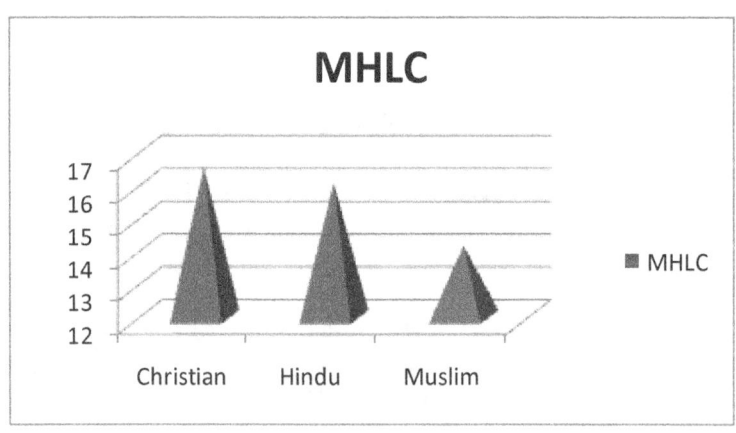

Figure 5

Difference of Males and Females of Whole social group.

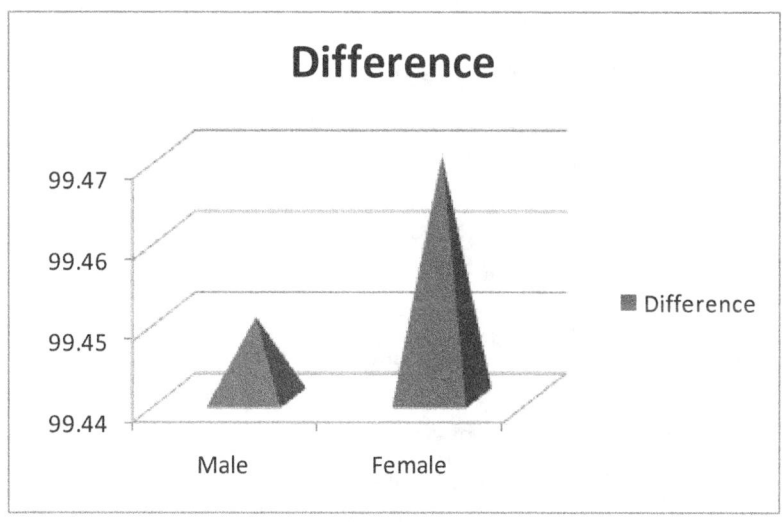

Figure 6

Male and Female from Christian, Muslim and Hindu group.

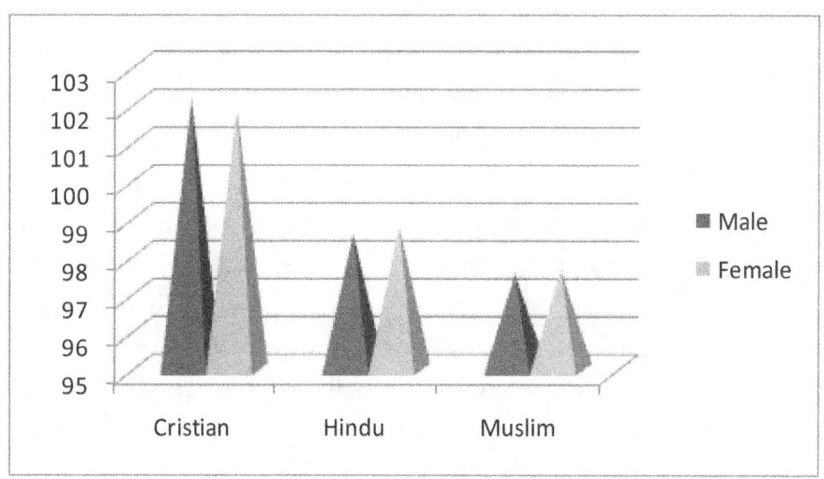

Figure 7

8. CONCLUSIONS

A. The most important conclusion of this research is there is no significant difference in religious life style of young social groups.

B. Only two groups (Hindu and Christians) have significant difference in factor of DUREL. Table2.1 indicates that Hindus have stronger religious life style than Christians.

C. Another notable conclusion of this research is that in all social groups all males and females have equal religious life style.

D. Last and final conclusion of my research is that modernization, development of science and technology, more and more use of internet, new fashion and films, widely spread media, these all factors have affected in peoples life style. So everybody believes in their own religion. Due to these all, every social group have equal, similar and effective religious life style.

9. SUGGESTIONS

After completion of this research work, I have found many fruitful useful and effective suggestions for world's young people.

A. Positive and strong religious attitude are very useful in every body's life.

B. Different social groups have equal. Life styles we all are basically human. Helping to each other everything.

C. Our society is deviated in different religion according to cast of people. Even though all the people having the similar religious life style. These things are proved by this research.

D. Final and important suggestion of researcher is that everybody has to believe in their own religion. Please worship pray to god every day. Religion will make your life happier and prosperous.

10. REFERENCES

Kenneth Shouler, "The Everything World's Religious: Explore The Beliefs", 2012

Emile Durkuim, "The Elementary Froms of the Religious Life", London, 2012

Johan Huizinga, "The Waning of the Middle Ages", New York, 1924

Koenig HG. 2001. Religion and medicine II: Religion, mental health, and related behaviors. *Int J Psychiatry Med.* 31:97-109.

Hill PC, et al. 2000. Conceptualizing religion and spirituality: Points of commonality, points of departure. *J Sci Study Relig.* 30:51-77

Pargament KI, et al. 2004. Religious coping methods as predictors of psychological, physical and spiritual outcomes among medically ill elderly patients: A two-year longitudinal study. *J Health Psychol.* 9:713-30.

Hill PC, Pargament KI. 2003. Advances in the conceptualization and measurement of religion and spirituality. Implications for physical and mental health research. *Am Psychol.* 58:64-74.

Koenig HG, Meador KG, Parkerson G, Religion index for psychiatric research: A 5-item measure for use in health outcome studies. *Am J Psychiatry.* 1997; 154:885-86.

Pargament KI, Koenig HG, Perez LM. 2000. The many methods of religious coping: Development and initial validation of the RCOPE. *J Clin Psychol.* 56:519-43.

Paloutizian RF, Ellison CW. 1982. *Loneliness, spiritual well-being and the quality of life*, in *Loneliness: A Sourcebook of Current Theory, Research and Therapy*, L.A. Peplau and D.Perlman, Editors. , Wiley-Interscience: New York. p. 224-37.

Wallston KA. 2005. The validity of the multidimensional health locus of control scales. *J Health Psychol.* 10:623-31.

Sherman AC, et al. 2001. Measuring religious faith in cancer patients: Reliability and construct validity of the Santa Clara Strength of Religious Faith Questionnaire. *Psycho oncology.* 10:436-43.

Boivin MJ, et al. 1999. *Spiritual Well-being Scale*, in *Measures of Religiosity*, P.C. Hill and R.W. Hood, Editors. Religious Education Press: Birmingham, AL.

http://en.wikipedia.org/wiki/Religion_in_India
http://en.wikipedia.org/wiki/Religion

ABOUT THE AUTHOR

Ankit Patel is an Indian Author, Storyteller, Novelist, Critic, Philosopher, Researcher and Counselor. He was born in Navamuvada, (Gujarat-India; 389230) to a middle class Gujarati family. His father is a farmer and his mother a government primary teacher. He writes as op-ed Articles for English, and Gujarati publications. Ankit is also editor for journals/magazine such as 'The International Journal of Indian Psychology' (Managing Editor) and 'International Journal of Engineering Research and Advanced Development' (Online Editor), where he writes about the mental health and youth development. He is also member of ResearchGate (Including 45 Nobel Laureates).